A SHORT MOTIVATIONAL DIARY TO MY PAST SELF

STAR LEWANDOWSKI

Star Lewandowski
A Short Motivational Diary to My Past Self

Cover design by **Mercedes Lewandowski**

Published by Spines
ISBN: 979-8-89383-061-3

In Loving Memory of my mother, who has always taught me how to be strong, independent and to follow my dreams.

This book is dedicated to my children and all the children of God who have struggled with insecurities and self-doubts. To all who have asked the question will I be, ok? This book is here to reassure you that you will be just fine.

The possibilities for your life have no limits.

PREFACE TO MY LIFE

Dear Diary,

I am writing to you to prepare you for the obstacles you will face as you embark on this journey we call Life. Remember, you will need all this information to help you navigate through the chapters of your Life. So, let us begin: You will grow up with two parents, one black and one white. Your Mother will be the matriarch of the family, but your father will be the backbone. Your Mother will be a strong, intelligent African American woman and your father will be a funny, intelligent Polish man. With this combo you are surely destined to have a breeze through life, right? I mean this is the best of both worlds. What could get better than this?

Well, hold on sister, I hate to be the bearer of sad news, but that's not how life works. Life will be smooth, just like a newly paved road, but then eventually there will be some cracks and may even some potholes that will cause you to have a blowout. Just like a car that rolls over a pothole repeatedly, it will cause severe damage to all parts of your vehicle, including components like shocks. So, you see these life potholes can cause some damage to the suspension, and when I say that I mean to the body. Your body, mind, and soul that keep you going will need some attention throughout this life's journey.

If you are ready then let's go for a ride, a ride of your life!

- Star

LIFE IS GREAT

As a young girl, you will grow up with your Mom and Dad in a house that had been previously owned by ancestors and then given to your father. This house will be more like a building. A building that was not like your typical traditional house, but it will be your home. A home that you will have throughout your childhood. In this home, you will create many memories. Some memories will be happy, and some will be sad. You will grow up with parents who learned to educate themselves and go back to school. Both parents will earn degrees. Even though they both will graduate from college, you will live in a low-middle-class home with your siblings. You will not have many material things or rarely even any money, but the one thing you will have will be each other. The material things and the money will not be important at the beginning of your childhood. You will not even realize that you are living a low-middle-class life. Your friends will be living similarly, so you will fit in financially with your peers, so need to panic right now.

You will be experiencing such innocence in this chapter of your life. Your mind will be so creative. Your imagination will be doing cartwheels in your brain with all the mental images that it is creating. *Can't* is not even in your vocabulary at this point, only *when, where*, and *what's next*.

Your life will be filled with joy. You will love your Barbies; your all-time favorite Barbie will be the Flo Jo (Florence Griffith Joyner) Barbie doll that was released. She was an Olympic athlete who won 3 Gold medals. You will enjoy this, Barbie. Cricket dolls, Cabbage Patch Kids, and get-in-shape girls with the cassette will be amazing. You will feel like you can carry out anything. You believe you can win a gold medal too. Life is good in Chapter 1 of your life.

2

MIDDLE SCHOOL IS TOUGH!

Ugh! Middle school will be a little tough on you. But I can promise you, you will get through it. You will attend a private catholic school that will be found on the west side in the inner city of Cleveland. You will develop PTSD and I say this to you because the present you will never forget all the times at school when there was a sock check or uniform check and you would have to raise your pants leg and your sock would have a little flower or something on it and you would have to wait in the office until a parent would come up to bring you a solid pair of socks or you could not be permitted to return to class. The only problem was your mom worked the night shift and was not getting up from her sleep after working all night to bring you a solid pair of socks to school and your dad worked days and was unable to do this. Your present you, will understand that this was unacceptable to be called out of classes for the entire day and realizing as a child this is something you did not even have control over. The present you will never forget this, it was like part of your life's foundation that will always stick with you. So, past you be ready for many days sitting in the office. The school will consist of a majority Caucasian and Hispanic population. There will be very few, and when I say very few African American and biracial children that will make up their demographics. You will feel like you are in constant survival mode. You will be trying to fit in with your peers, but you will know that you are different from the constant reminders of your classmates and your friends. They will call you names about your looks that you have no control over, like big lips, big eyes, nappy hair and ugly. You will not have the flowy straight hair, you will not have a flat booty, and you will not have small lips, which back then was so popular. How ironic all these things are desired during the present time and are even being bought by many women. I mean women are risking their lives for this. So, to the past me, you already have it, girl!

Just be patient and watch and see. This I guarantee will not fail you. No purchasing or fillers here. Let us just say you are ahead of your time. God and sports will get you through these tough times. You will turn to God every chance you get, and man will the sports toughen you up.

This my dear is how you will survive. You will learn to defend yourself. Your skin starts to thicken. You start realizing how to fight back and I am not just saying physically but I must warn you that you will get into a physical altercation on the playground due to some racial slurs that were said to you. You win this physical battle but, in your present, you realize that you won the battle, but you lost the war. You will learn in your present time that this could have been managed differently with a touch of class. But heck you sure did feel good this day to conquer this bully! You will walk off this playground into the office with your head high and knowing that phone call to your parents was coming but you know God got you, you know he knows your heart.

I must tell you though that through all that you will make some lifelong friends that you are still friends with presently. These friends are not friends you have to see every day, or heck even talk to every month, but one thing is for sure girl they got your back if you call them. These are your childhood besties! You will forever keep them close.

3

HIGH SCHOOL, HERE I COME

LET'S GO! You will now have your high school years. This will be an adventure with a lot of fun memories and some sad ones too. You will continue to play sports throughout your high school years. You will learn to be a part of a team at a high school level. Bonds will be made, friendships will grow, and boys will be present, so get ready homegirl, there is no turning back. This is real. You begin your high school journey as a freshman at a private catholic school. Be prepared for your first day as a freshman. It will be an experience you will never forget. It's roll-call! In case you do not know, that means it's time for attendance. Yes, you will be present, or at least you think you are.

There will be a short older Caucasian nun with glasses and gray hair who will call your name. And yes! You are so excited and you will shout out with confidence as you raise your hand saying, "Here!" because you know you have your first high school question answer right; but *boy* brace yourself, you may be moving too fast girl. Your heart will begin to beat faster and you will feel yourself panicking as the nun yells out to you that you are lying and she will not have this in her classroom. You will begin to question," Did she say my name? How could I have gotten this wrong? Oh, No!" But you are correct, and she will say it again and repeatedly you will say, "Here, I am present", with your hand raised. The kids in the classroom will be laughing but relax get it together and do not panic as she starts to yell, "Get out of my class and go to the office, this is a Polish last name, and you are not Polish!" You will try to explain to her, as to your white friend from middle school, who also is your classmate in high school, your life and background to them. Still, you will be told to leave and go to the principal's office for lying in her classroom. You will get up and walk out while listening to all the heckling and laughter.

This my past me is your high school experience of racism by your educator. Yes, your parents entrusted this institution to help guide and prepare you through your journey we call life. You will get through this and will be allowed back in the classroom, but you will feel different. Different is starting to feel like your norm.

All that said, you and your family will eventually move out of state and you will have to attend a new high school… but trust me, you will have a wonderful time. Honestly, one of your best high school experiences. Oh yeah, boyfriends will not be hard for you to have in High School. Girl, you are the catch and don't even know it. You don't even realize how gorgeous you are. *Sheesh*! I wish the present me would have known this in the past. You are compassionate, caring, beautiful, and intelligent! My dear, you are a child of God for real and he may have given you a little extra too!

The present me is loving the past me, so just give me a moment to take this all in, as I forgot to before. Ok, I am ready. You will eventually move back to your home state and yes you will graduate High School!

4

I'M ON MY OWN

KNOCK, Knock! Let the games begin. At this point in your life, you think the world is not ready for you, but low and behold: You realize that you are not ready for the world. Ready, set, here I come.

After high school, you will attend a small college close to home and stay in a dorm. You will continue to play sports in college. You are officially on your own. No one will wake you up or tell you to go to class or do your homework; this, here, is all you, ready or not. This honestly was not hard for you. You are a natural-born leader. Things were going great but at home, the stress of your mom being sick is weighing on you. Your mom's illness begins to feel like your illness. You truly are an empath. You begin to take on your mother's issues and stress, and it consumes your life.

You decide to leave school. The stress was too much to bear. It began to be too hard to concentrate away from home.

22

5

COMMUNITY COLLEGE

COMMUNITY COLLEGE WILL SAVE YOU. You decide to enroll in the community college and enter their nursing program, which will set the tone for your future and how you will support your family once you have one. That will take place in Chapter 6 of your life. You will graduate and start your nursing career. Things are great until they are not. Money will be good for a person with no real responsibilities other than taking care of themselves. You will eventually start a relationship and with that, you will get 3 amazing blessings that your present you would not change for the world.

Present you still have a hard time understanding why God chose you to bring these beautiful blessings into this world, but I guess he knew you could get the job done, you could do this for life.

Thank you, God, for all the 5 blessings that I later will have. Ok, so let's keep moving past me because the present me can't wait to see you get to me.

24

RELATIONSHIPS

BE ready for some not-so-good relationships. Your relationship with the father of your 3 children will end, but wait! Love will find you again. Pay close attention my dear when I say *Love will FIND you again* or so you will think it is love again that keeps popping up. You will get blessed with 2 more Blessings and you will think, *Wow God loves me! I have five now.*

You will get married and divorced! You will experience a lot of traumas from your relationships that will have a lot to do with how the present you will become. You will have to learn to be a single parent. You will know that this is foreign to you because you were raised in a two-parent household that showed love and support to their children, but you know that you will have to do this alone.

You are smart, and strong, you got this. You know that people want you to fail. Society has already labeled you as a statistic of a single-parent household who was going to live in poverty. This my dear will be fuel for you. So, let's keep it moving, we are almost there!

7

HOME

At this point, you have already bought the home that you have been living in with your children for some time. You will be struggling to make ends meet. Father Number One has been out of the picture for many years. Let us just say he was absent during your children's whole childhood, but it will be ok. You will lose your mom to health issues and this will be tough. You have adapted to this life as a single parent, but you never really have accepted it. I mean, you will hurt, you will cry, but the one certain thing is that you will never give up. That kind of talk is not allowed in your household.

You will eventually have another pothole that life has placed in your path, but this one is a deep pothole. This one only God can get you out. Breaking News: Your baby father # 2 will be tragically killed, which will be ruled a homicide. You got it! Your life's suspension is bad, just like a car. It will feel unbalanced and unstable, which can cause you to lose control of your car but even worse… this is your life! No more wheels on the ground and riding smoothly, you are hitting all bumps! Time to take this car or life in to get checked out. Maintenance is needed once again.

YOU MADE IT

YOU MADE IT! *Sheesh*! That was a rough ride, but we are riding a smooth course now.

You have a sophomore in college at The Ohio State University, who has a drive on life that has no speed limit, let's just say it's limitless. The only thing she knows is she is going to make it! Make all her dreams come true. OH-IO. All of you Ohio State alums and fans will understand that. You have a star athlete who is a Senior in high school and you cannot wait to see all the amazing things God has in store for him.

You have an entrepreneur junior in high school who created his clothing brand. I mean, this kid is working with clothing manufacturing companies and everything, you go boy!

You have a personal 12-year-old chef… man, can't wait for your restaurant to open.

You have a 10-year-old mathematician. This kid is bright, and intelligent beyond his years.

Finally, you! You did it and are still doing it. You are a private Nurse, working with VIP clients, a Life Coach, a mentor, a motivational speaker, an author, and a mom. You have probably read every self-help book and personal development book that's out there, just to make sure you were good. Good with what you need to know to help you in life, you know that is all part of life's maintenance you need to help you continue to have growth. You will continue to keep educating your mind with books, seminars, and simply uplifting people's advice and stories.

The saying goes, "Your mind is a terrible thing to waste", they aren't lying. You truly understand that without the many talks with God and the countless prayers, you would not be here today and blessed to watch your kids grow and for yourself to continue to grow and pursue all your dreams and goals and most importantly execute them. I will forever be grateful and will continue my pursuit of happiness and serve others as a child of God.

EPILOGUE

Life is like a car, it will need constant maintenance and tune-ups, or it can go bad. Past me, you will get through it. Words of advice to me, always continue to work on yourself. Your life's possibilities are limitless. Dream of a little dream. In the words of Theodore Roosevelt, "Dreams are a dime a dozen. It's their execution that counts", And as my young, entrepreneur son always says, "Make it Happen!" To all who went on this reverse ride to my past with me, thank you.

WORDS OF WISDOM

What I have learned on this ride to the past is that how and where we grow up and who we grow up with does have an impact on our life. It is our foundation that we have no control over. It's ultimately what we are born and raised in to. But with this knowledge, I have learned that we do have control over how we design it. So, just like a car, you can purchase it with a few dents and maybe a few missing pieces, but under the hood you know there is an amazing running engine. You know you have all the tools and resources needed to put some work into it and design it how you want. You have a vision of how you want it to be. It's kind of like life. You get to create your own success by the choices you make and by the company you keep. Always remember your life is ultimately yours to design..

In closing, I want to say to all my children of God in this world, always remember to invest in you. Put more investment in yourself than you do in your job or the companies you work for. This I guarantee will always get you the gold. So go for the win, you are worth it. For all those people who have have had some cracks and hit some pot holes in life, remember you will be ok.

Jesus looked to them and said, "With man this is impossible, but with God all things are possible."

— MATTHEW 19:26

WHAT ARE SOME OF YOUR GOALS?

1.

____

2.

____

3.

____

4.

____

5.

____

6.

____

7.

____

8.

____

9.

____

10.

____

WHAT ARE SOME THINGS THAT YOU ARE DOING TO ACHIEVE THESE GOALS?

ARE THESE GOALS GOING TO
HELP YOU BE A BETTER PERSON?
WRITE DOWN HOW YOU THINK
THESE GOALS WILL HELP YOU BE
A BETTER PERSON.

HOW ARE THESE GOALS GOING TO HELP YOU SERVE OTHERS?

WHEN DO YOU WANT THESE GOALS ACHIEVED?

THINK OF THREE PEOPLE YOU WANT TO THANK AND WRITE THEM DOWN.

1. _______________________________________

2. _______________________________________

3. _______________________________________

NOW, GO AND TELL THEM THANK YOU!